# Contents

# Introduction

Many bizarre and gruesome creatures roam the world of mythology. Although their origins may be lost in the mists of history, they have preyed on people's superstitions and imaginations since ancient times. No creatures have struck greater fear than werewolves and other shapeshifters. Caught precariously between the worlds of human and beast, they have filled people with terror for centuries and given rise to countless chilling myths and legends, told around the world. In modern times, they have featured in films, fiction, fairytales, and as characters in comics and computer games. Are you ready to go over to the dark side? It will send shivers down your spine...

# Werewolves
## and Other Shapeshifters

A book of monstrous beings from the dark side of myths and legends around the world, illustrated by David West and written by Anita Ganeri

*This edition published in 2012 by Wayland*

Wayland
Hachette Children's Books
338 Euston Road
London NW1 3BH

Wayland Australia
Level 17/207 Kent Street
Sydney, NSW 2000

Produced by

**David West ⚲ Children's Books**
7 Princeton Court
55 Felsham Road
London SW15 1AZ

*Designer:* David West
*Editor:* Katharine Pethick
*Illustrator:* David West

A CIP catalogue record for this book is available from the British Library.

ISBN: 9780750267793

*Printed in* China

Wayland is a division of Hachette Children's Books
an Hachette UK company
www.hachette.co.uk

Picture credits:
5t, luc legay; 5m, goldmund100; 5b, Vall; 30 both, coolisandsong24

# Werewolves

A snarling beast, fleet of foot, cunning as a fox, and boasting huge claws, a muzzle full of foul teeth, and supernatural strength – this is the terrifying werewolf, roaming the countryside in search of prey.

Wolves were hunted because they attacked farmers' livestock.

A werewolf is a creature that can be human or wolf – sometimes changing at will, sometimes under the control of another force. It is the best-known of the shapeshifters. Most werewolf myths come from medieval times, and from countries where packs of wild wolves roamed the countryside and often carried away villagers to eat.

The earliest werewolf tale comes from the classical mythology of ancient Greece. King Lycaon tries to feed a dead child to the god Zeus, who is angry and turns Lycaon into a werewolf.

A German print made in 1711 appears to show a werewolf in mid transformation.

# Becoming a Werewolf

*So how does an unfortunate human become a werewolf in the first place? And once a werewolf, how do they trigger their gruesome transformation from human form to wolf form?*

Modern books and films often show people becoming werewolves after being bitten or scratched by another werewolf. In mythology, werewolves are created in other ways. Common methods include sleeping outdoors during a full moon, being born under a full moon, and being cursed by a witch. Lycanthropy (the transformation of a human into a wolf) can also be passed from one generation to the next because of a family curse.

*Arching his back in excruciating pain, a werewolf grows a muzzle of sharp teeth, body hair, pointed ears, powerful muscles and huge claws as he shapeshifts into a wolf.*

Folklore in South America tells that the seventh son born into a family becomes a werewolf (sometimes seventh children were abandoned or killed just because of this).

Putting on a wolf-skin belt, or better still an entire wolf skin, seems to be the most popular method for a werewolf to change from human to wolf. When the wolf skin is removed, the process is reversed. Ointments made from ingredients such as nightshade (a poisonous plant) and bat's blood, and rubbed on the body, also start the transformation off. Another trigger is to drink from a puddle in the footprint of a real wolf, or from a stream that a real wolf has drunk from. A werewolf may spend hours or days in wolf form.

A drawing entitled *Werewolves*, drawn in 1512 by Lucas Altere the Elder, shows the terrifying result of a werewolf attack.

# Werewolf features

*Both in human and wolf form, werewolves are said to have features of the opposite form that allow them to be recognised.*

While in human form werewolves are believed to have some strange wolf-like features. These include pale, rough skin, bushy eyebrows that grow to meet in the middle, hair on the face, hands and feet, pointed ears, and long, red fingernails shaped like almonds. One medieval theory was that werewolves wore their wolf skin inside out, with the hair on the inside. Some unfortunate werewolf suspects were cut open to test this theory.

*Etchings from a 1667 book 'Miraculous Nature' appear to show male and female werewolves.*

Iconismus . IV. Ponatur è regione pag. 395.

Fig. I Puella pilosa filia annorum duodecim.

Fig. II. Puella pilosa Filia altera annorum octo.

*The human eyes of a werewolf behind the face of a wolf.*

While in wolf form, mythical werewolves often looked and moved just like real wolves, but they could speak and had human eyes. Other reports tell of werewolves that were half man, half wolf. Any wound inflicted on a werewolf in wolf form would remain when it returned to human form – a useful clue for werewolf hunters.

*A scene of a werewolf attack from an 1865 book 'The Book of Were-Wolves: Being an Account of a Terrible Superstition'. Once in wolf form, a werewolf presented a terrifying shadowy figure that moved swiftly through the countryside.*

# Warding off Werewolves

*According to myths, there are various ways to save yourself from a werewolf attack, which are similar to methods of warding off other evil creatures. There are also ways of curing and even killing werewolves.*

Traditionally, objects made from the metals iron and silver can be used to ward off an approaching werewolf. Throwing an iron or silver object over a werewolf's head will stop it. Scalding a werewolf with boiling water is also thought to work.

A few types of plants were supposed to stop a werewolf in its tracks, so surrounding a house or campsite with these plants would keep werewolves away during the night. The plants included rye, mistletoe and wolfsbane. In Belgium, mountain ash was thought to work, too.

According to Greek and Roman myths, keeping a werewolf on the move until it was exhausted would cure it. In medieval Europe, hitting a werewolf on the head three times with a metal knife, piercing its hands with nails, or calling it by its Christian name three times might do the trick. Killing a werewolf was not easy. You needed to destroy its heart or brain, or shoot it with a silver bullet or arrow. The beast would always return to human form before death.

Aconitum Lycocto, num flore Delphinij.

Aconitum Lycoctonum flore luteo.

*Wolfsbane is a popular name for the herb Aconitum. It has been used for centuries both as a medicine and a poison. It was thought to cause lycanthropy if eaten, but could also repel werewolves.*

In Denmark it was believed that boiling water would scare off a werewolf.

# Werewolves in Europe

*Europe is undoubtedly the world's werewolf hotspot. Here, werewolf myths come from a time when real wolves roamed the length and breadth of the continent, from France to Russia, and Norway to Spain.*

In the Middle Ages, wolves terrorised rural villages and towns throughout Europe, especially when food was in short supply. Every country has its own word for the werewolf – in Iceland it is varulfur, in Italy, lupo mannero, in Lithuania, vilkatas. But werewolf tales are rare in Britain, where wolves had been hunted to extinction by early medieval times.

In France, a werewolf is known as a loup-garou (say 'lu-ga-ru'). Perhaps France's most famous werewolf case was of the Beast of Gevaudan. The case began in 1764 with the first of a series of beastly attacks and murders. Terrified survivors spoke of a massive red creature with huge teeth that ran at great speed. Rumours of a werewolf continued even when a huge wolf was trapped and killed.

*The Wolf of Chazes was shot and killed in 1765. It was suspected of being the Beast of Gevaudan. It is displayed here at the court of King Louis XV.*

*The wolf of Ansbach was believed to be a werewolf. It was chased into a well, killed and hung from a gibbet.*

At his trial in Paris in 1598 for the murder of a child, Jacques Rollet admitted that his hands and feet became those of a wolf before he attacked the child. He used ointment to cause the change. Germany's most famous werewolf was Peter Stubbe. Legend says that Stubbe became a wolf and attacked and killed local people. He was finally captured and confessed to becoming a werewolf by wearing a wolf-skin belt. Stubbe was executed in 1589.

*The story of Little Red Riding Hood may have had its roots in werewolf myths.*

# Werewolves Around the World

Although Europe is the main source of werewolf myths, there are werewolf stories from many other parts of the world. Some even originate in places where there have never been real wolves.

In North America, where wolves still roam today, werewolf myths are quite common. In eastern Canada, myths about loup-garou in the forests around Quebec were brought from France by colonists, and were mixed with Native American beliefs. The French also spread their werewolf myths to Haiti and other Caribbean islands, and to the area around New Orleans, USA.

A wolf helmet made by the Tlingit people of Alaska, who admired the wolf's strength and hunting skills.

The Crow Indians believed that a spirit in the form of a werewolf lived in Big Horn Canyon, and would eat any human that ventured there.

Native North American people have their own werewolf tales to tell. The Algonquian people, a group made up of many Native American tribes, believe in an evil spirit known as the wendigo. It could turn people into gluttonous, flesh-eating, werewolf-like creatures, looking like skeletons with skin on. The Navajo people thought that witches took the form of wolves, known as Mai-Cob.

In South America, particularly in Argentina, it was believed that if seven sons were born in a row to a family, the seventh would become a werewolf (or lobizon) and would wander the mountains, eating dead animals in between attacking humans.

**Haiti** The Jé-rouge ('red eyes') is a spirit that possesses people, turning them into werewolf-like, man-eating creatures.

**Brazil** Portuguese settlers to South America brought with them myths of the werewolf, or lobisomem.

**Mexico** The nahual is a werewolf that steals cheese and attacks women, and can also become a cat, eagle or bull.

**Philippines** The aswang is a part vampire, part werewolf that feeds on human flesh.

**North Africa** The boudas is a type of sorcerer that can be transformed into a werehyena.

*A lobizon drags an unfortunate victim into the shadows of an Argentinian town.*

# Other Shapeshifters

There are many other mythical creatures that make terrible transformations. The Romanian strigoi is a blood-sucking zombie that can change into many different animals such as barn owls, bats, rats, cats, wolves, dogs, snakes, and toads.

Daphne, a nymph in Greek mythology transformed herself into a tree to escape the god Apollo.

In Norse mythology, Fafnir shapeshifted from a dwarf into a dragon, the symbol of greed, to guard a hoard of gold.

Tales of shapeshifters come from countries all over the world. Many are 'were' beasts – humans who change into animal form just as werewolves change into wolf form, and carry out horrifying attacks on victims. Among them are werecats, such as the werejaguar of Central America and the weretiger of India, weresnakes in China, werecrocodiles in Africa, and werebears in Scandinavia. Vampires were thought to transform into bats or wolves.

In mythology, gods, witches, wizards, sorcerers and fairies often have the power of shapeshifting. They may take up the shape of almost any animal they choose.

# Werecats

*The werecat is the feline equivalent of the werewolf. Werecats feature in the mythology of countries where lions, tigers, leopards and other big cats roam.*

Weretiger myths are common throughout Asia. No doubt the myths are linked to real tiger attacks on people. In China, the victims of curses became weretigers, as did the ghosts of real tigers.

In Thailand, a tiger that killed lots of people during its mortal life was thought to become a weretiger when it died.

In India, a weretiger was thought to be a sorcerer who could take tiger form. Indian weretigers apparently attacked and killed cattle, and often stalked and savaged villagers.

In Indonesia, a weretiger takes up its big-cat shape at night to protect its livestock and crops. It rarely attacks humans unless it is ravenously hungry or seeking revenge.

*Asian weretiger*

A fearsome werejaguar leaps from the undergrowth of a jungle.

The werejaguar was a supernatural creature that terrorised the people of ancient civilisations of Mesoamerica (modern-day southern Mexico and northern Central America) – including the Olmecs, Maya and Aztecs. A werejaguar was said to transform from human form to jaguar form by putting on the skin of a real jaguar. Many priests and shamans were supposed to be werejaguars. Images of werejaguars are common in art of the time, especially the art of the Olmecs.

*An Olmec stone carving of a part human, part jaguar, made sometime between 1000 BC and 300 BC.*

Some African peoples believed in lion and leopard gods and goddesses, which took human form and also transformed into lions and leopards. The children of these gods and goddesses become werelions or wereleopards. Other African peoples believed that members of their royal families became werelions when they died.

*Aztec warriors believed that dressing in jaguar skins gave them the edge in battle. This image comes from the Codex Magliabechiano, an Aztec religious document.*

# Skin-walkers and Berserkers

*Of all the shapeshifters, none can be more terrifying than the cunning skin-walkers of North American legend and the crazed beserkers of Norse myths.*

In Native American legends, a skin-walker is a person who can transform into any animal at will. The crow, the fox, the wolf and the coyote are common forms. A skin-walker takes the form of the animal that is most useful at the time – for example, it might become a crow to gain a bird's-eye view of the land below. Skin-walkers would knock on the doors and windows of houses, terrifying those inside.

In Norse myth, a berserker is a warrior who puts on the skin of a bear (or sometimes a wolf), which transforms him into a fighter with superhuman strength and speed. The word berserker comes from the Old Norse words ber (meaning bear) and serkr

*The Hombre Caiman (or Alligator Man) of Colombian folklore is a fisherman turned into an alligator.*

(meaning coat), and the English word berserk derives from it. A beserker fought as though in a terrible rage, striking and biting his enemies, and howling ferociously like a wolf, but he could not be harmed himself.

*A bronze plate found on the Swedish island of Öland. It shows a Viking warrior and a berserker. In reality, berserkers may have fought under the influence of drink or drugs.*

Skin-walkers moved so fast that they were almost impossible to catch. Bullets had no effect on them.

# Swan Maidens and Selkies

A repeating theme in shapeshifting mythology is an animal that transforms into human form by removing its skin. The creature then appears in the shape of a young woman.

*In the Old Norse poem Volundarkvida three brothers marry the swan maidens they see bathing.*

The swan maiden features in Norse myths. By removing its skin, a swan maiden transforms from a swan to a young woman. The transformation is reversed by putting the skin back on, or sometimes by dressing in clothes with swan feathers attached. In some stories a young man steals the swan maiden's skin while she is in human form, and she marries him so that she can recover her skin.

*Selkies rose from the sea and danced on the shore. Like swan maidens they sometimes had to marry men who took and hid their seal skins.*

Myths that originated in the Orkneys and Shetlands (islands off northern Scotland) describe the selkie, a creature from the sea that sheds its skin to turn from seal form to human form. The selkie must put its seal skin back on to return to seal form. The selkie may only be seen by one human, and only for a short time before it must return to the sea. Similar myths come from the Faroe Islands, Iceland and Ireland, where seals are often seen.

In Africa, the buffalo-maiden is a buffalo that shapeshifts into a young woman. In China, the fox spirit often appears as a girl. Similar myths come from Korea and Japan, where the fox spirit is called a kitsune.

*The Japanese kitsune casts a fox-shaped shadow even when in human form.*

# Shapeshifter Gods

*Myths from ancient Greece and other ancient civilisations describe gods, goddesses and demons who change shape to gain an advantage in combat, to play tricks and to find love.*

In Greek mythology, Zeus took on the form of different animals, including a cuckoo, a swan and a bull, to visit goddesses and mortal women. Proteus was known as The Old Man of the Sea. He knew all things, including the future. He would only reveal his secrets to someone who tied him down, which was tricky as Proteus would take the shape of different animals to escape.

*The ancient Egyptian god Seth took many animal forms.*

In Norse mythology Loki is the companion of Odin, god of war. He is a troublemaker who has the ability to change shape, and become any animal. In Hindu mythology, a naga is a being that is half human, half god who can appear in human or serpent form. In Hindu art, nagas are shown as multi-headed cobras or as creatures with a human head and a coiled serpent body.

*In Greek mythology, Europa is carried off to Crete by the god Zeus, disguised in the form of a white bull.*

In Homer's Odyssey, Proteus shapeshifts into a lion to escape the clutches of Menelaus.

# Punished

Gods, goddesses, the Devil, witches, wizards and sorcerers have often used shapeshifting as a form of punishment. Victims were changed into a whole host of terrible creatures, normally to remain in that form for the rest of their days – or even for all eternity.

A Greek vase showing Circe transforming Odysseus's men into wild pigs.

In Homer's Odyssey, the goddess Athena took on many forms. She was also the goddess of handicrafts. When Arachne challenged her to a weaving contest, she changed Arachne into a spider. Artemis, the Greek goddess of wild animals, transformed Actaeon, a Greek hero, into a stag because he saw her bathing. Circe was a Greek sorceress with the power to change people into animals. She transformed Odysseus's men into pigs when they landed on her island.

The goddess Artemis turned Actaeon into a stag. Actaeon's dogs then tore him to pieces.

Odin transformed Svipdag into a sea-dragon because Svipdag had angered him. Later, Svipdag's wife, Freya, tried to rescue him but she could not break Odin's spell.

In Russia, legend describes the wawkalak, a person turned into a werewolf by the Devil as a punishment. Saint Patrick is said to have made Vereticus, a Welsh king, into a wolf after Vereticus rejected Christianity. In Norse legend, Loki, companion of the gods Odin and Thor, was punished for killing Odin's son. Odin turned one of Loki's sons into a wolf, which promptly ate Loki's other son. Odin also turned the hero Svipdag into a dragon.

*Being transformed into a spider was the fate of the weaver Arachne, who angered the goddess Athena.*

# Glossary

**Berserk** Go into a frenzy of violent or destructive behaviour.

**Classical** To do with the ancient Greeks and Romans, and their civilisation.

**Colonists** People who settle in a place far from their homeland but which may be ruled by their homeland.

**Confessed** Told the truth about something.

**Coyote** A dog-like animal that lives in the deserts and prairies of North America.

**Etchings** Drawings made on metal or glass, using acid or a sharp instrument.

**Executed** Put to death.

**Extinction** When animals or plants die out for ever.

**Gluttonous** Greedy, with a big appetite.

**Legends** Traditional stories, often based on supposedly historical events.

**Lycanthropy** The supposed transformation of a human into a wolf.

**Medieval** Relating to the Middle Ages, a period of European history from around the 5th – 15th century AD.

**Mortal** Living things that do not live for ever but eventually die.

**Myths** Traditional stories, not based in historical fact but using supernatural characters to explain human behaviour and natural events.

**Nymph** A spirit in the form of a beautiful girl in Greek mythology.

**Prey** Animals that are hunted by other animals for food.

**Repel** Force back or drive back.

**Sorcerer** A person who uses magical powers. Another word for a witch or wizard.

**Supernatural** Magical beings, such as fairies and ghosts, and unexplained events.

**Vampire** A bat-like creature that rises from a grave at night to drink its victims' blood.

**Zombie** A supernatural spirit that brings a dead body back to life.

# Further Reading

Ganeri, Anita. *An Illustrated Guide to Mythical Creatures.* Brighton: Book House, 2009.

McCall, Gerrie. *Monsters and Villains of the Movies and Literature.* London: Scholastic, 2008.

Oxlade, Chris. *Can Science Solve the Mystery of Vampires and Werewolves?* Oxford: Heinemann Library, 2008.

Rissman, Rebecca. *Werewolves.* Oxford: Raintree, 2010.

Tonge, Peter. *Truly Monstrous Tales: Werewolves.* London: Hodder Children's Books, 1999.

*Werewolf attacking a man, from a 15th century German work.*

# Index

*The Werewolf of Eschenbach, Germany 1685*